ALL ABachelorsBelugas

WRITTEN BY
Jordan Hoffman

Belugas are mammals. Muskoxen, walruses, and humans are other types of mammals.

Belugas belong to the same family as narwhals. Belugas are sometimes called white whales.

Belugas grow to between 2.6 and 4.5 metres long.

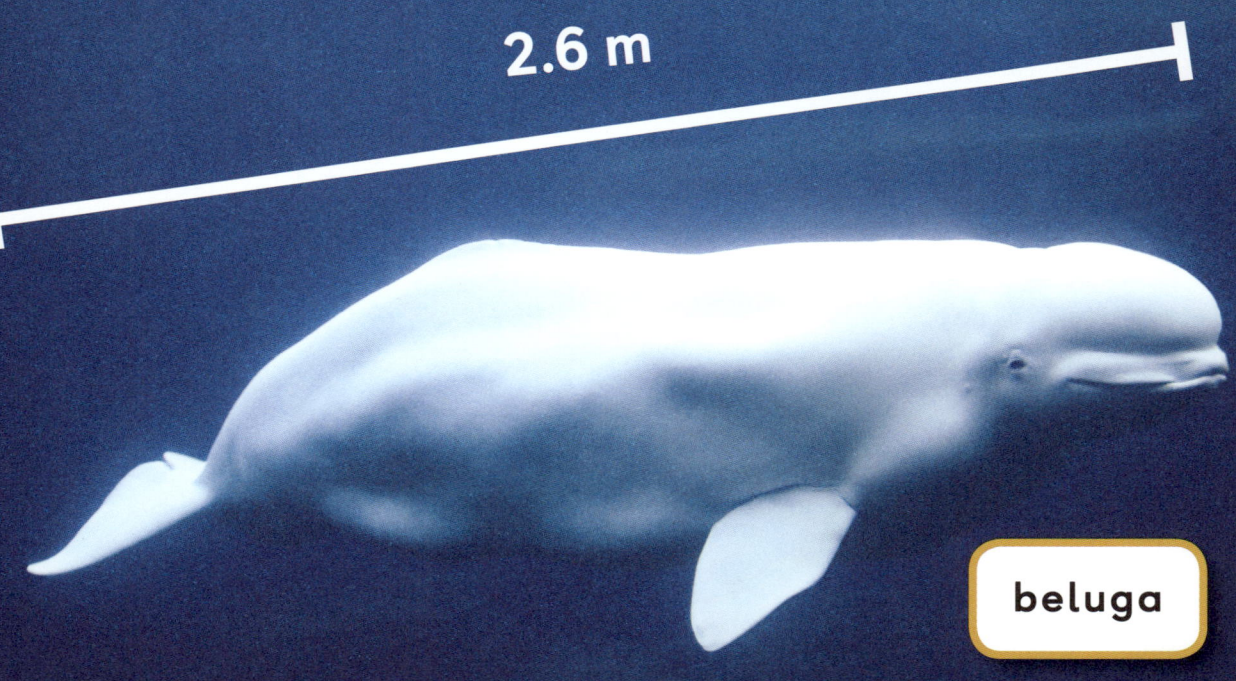

2.6 m

beluga

Belugas can weigh up to 1900 kilograms. That is heavier than a polar bear!

Females are usually shorter and weigh less than males.

Adult belugas have all-white skin. The skin and outer **blubber** layer of belugas is called *maktaaq* in Inuktitut. Maktaaq can be up to 15 centimetres thick. The blubber layer helps keep belugas warm.

Maktaaq is a good source of nutrition for people living in the Canadian Arctic.

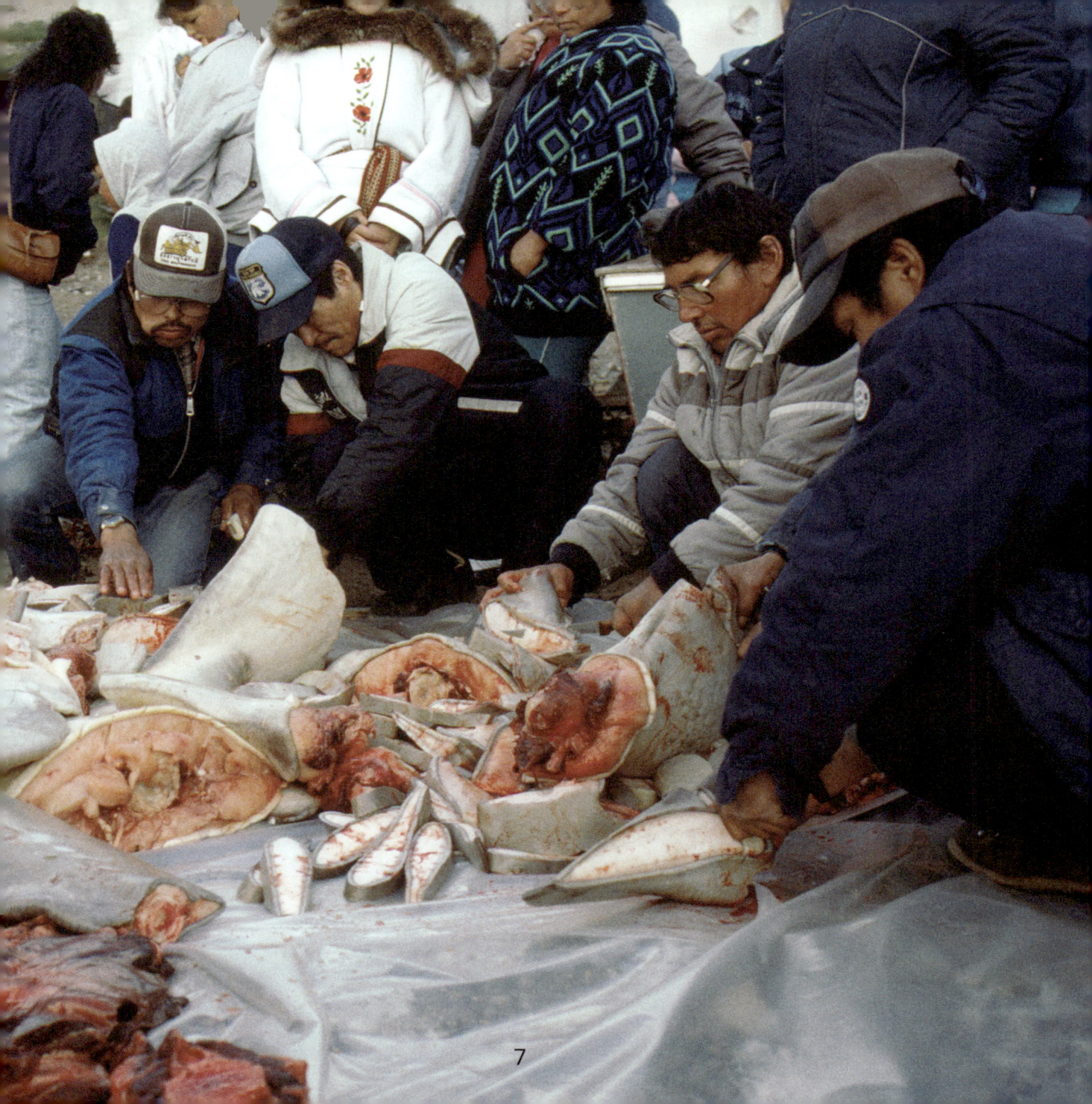

Most parts of a beluga's body are covered in blubber, but not their head, tail, and flippers. These parts that are not covered in blubber are small compared to other whales, so belugas don't lose as much heat.

Belugas also have long, flexible necks. They can move their heads easily as they swim.

Belugas have a bulb on their foreheads. This bulb is called a melon.

Unlike most whales and dolphins, belugas can make different facial expressions. They do this by changing the shape of their melon and mouth. These facial expressions might help belugas communicate with each other.

Unlike many whales and dolphins, belugas do not have a fin on their back. This probably helps them travel through water covered in ice. They can also break through thin ice by swimming up and pushing on the ice with their back.

Belugas live underwater in the **marine environment**. In Nunavut, they are found near communities such as Panniqtuuq, Kimmirut, Grise Fiord, and Arviat, among others.

Most belugas are found in the Arctic. There is also one small population living on the east coast of Canada in the Gulf of Saint Lawrence.

Belugas are **predators**. They eat fish, including Arctic cod, turbot, and Arctic char. They also eat **crustaceans**, such as shrimp and mollusks.

Arctic char

shrimp

Belugas are a food source for polar bears and orcas. Polar bears can hunt belugas when they get trapped in ice, and orcas can hunt belugas in open water.

polar bear

orca

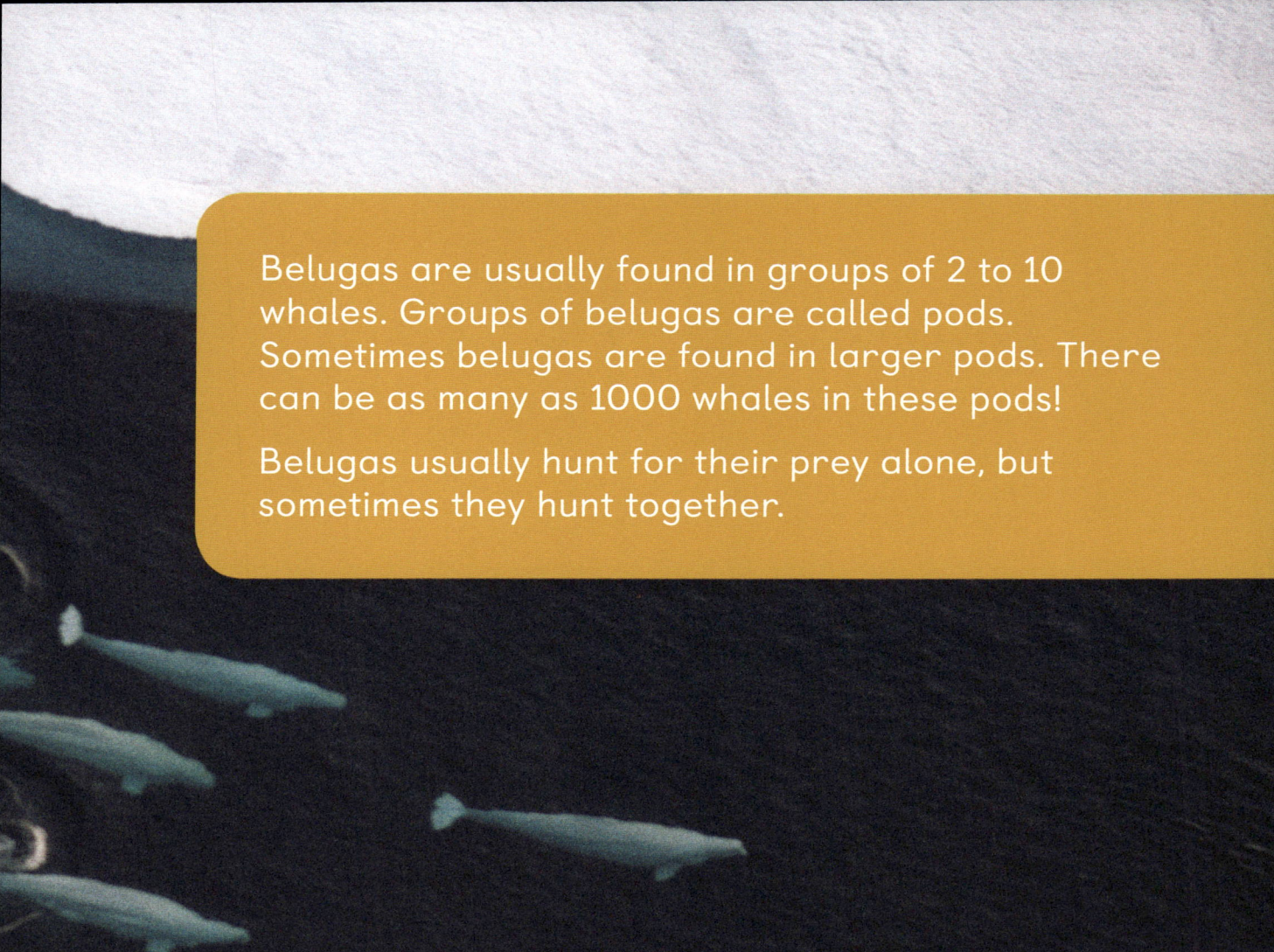

Belugas are usually found in groups of 2 to 10 whales. Groups of belugas are called pods. Sometimes belugas are found in larger pods. There can be as many as 1000 whales in these pods!

Belugas usually hunt for their prey alone, but sometimes they hunt together.

Belugas make sounds to help them communicate with other belugas. These sounds are called chirps, whistles, and squeals. Some belugas can produce over 50 different types of these sounds!

Belugas also use clicks and buzz-like sounds to find prey. The sounds bounce off fish and other things in the environment.

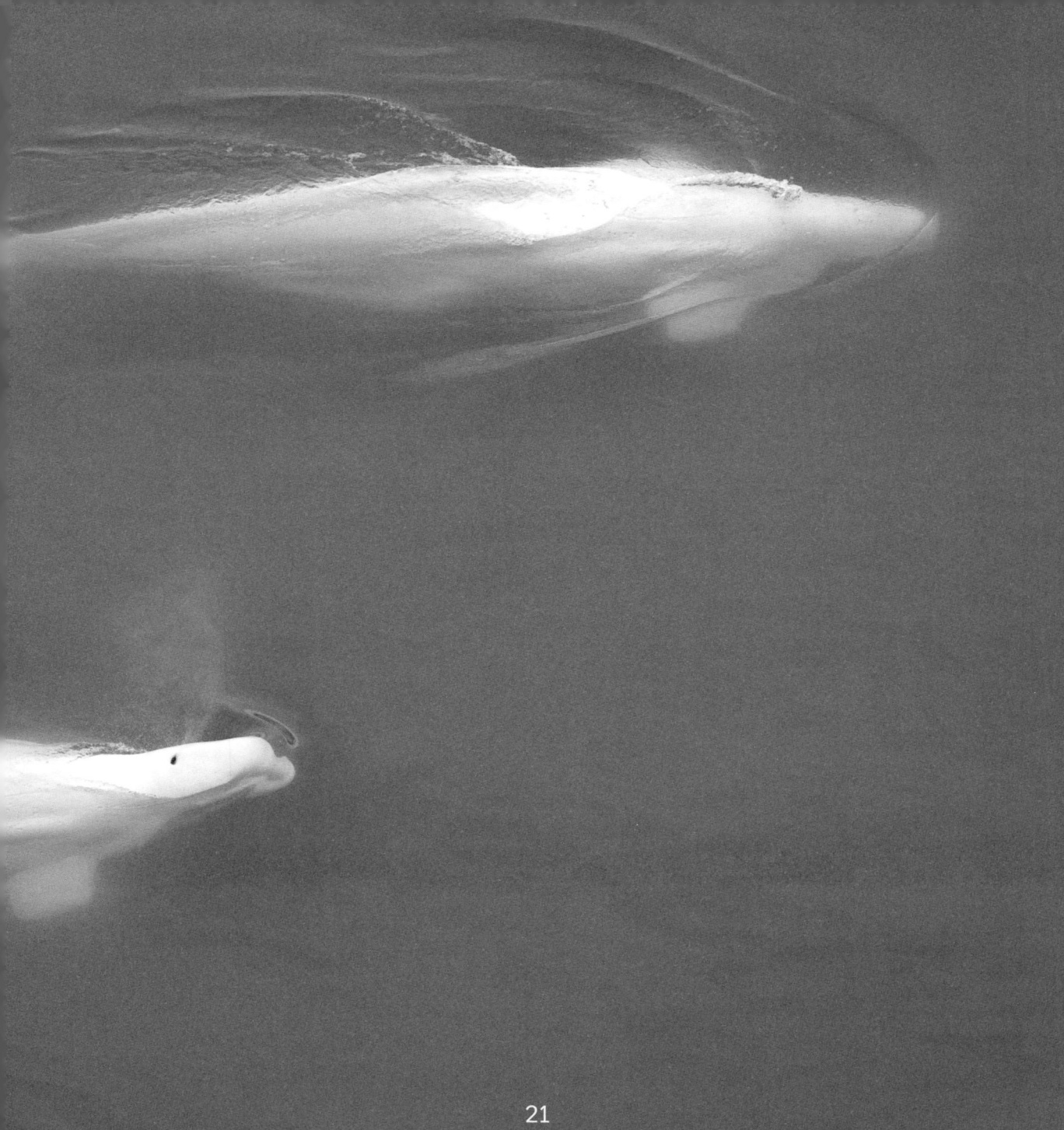

Young belugas are called calves. Females have their first calves when they are six or seven years old. When calves are born, they stay with their mothers for two to three years.

Calves are born with grey skin. Their skin turns lighter as they grow older. They can take up to eight years to turn fully white.

Belugas can be found in different areas at different times of the year.

In spring, they are often found at the floe edge or in large cracks in the ice called leads.

In summer, belugas are found along the coast and in shallow waters.

In autumn, belugas **migrate** to areas with deeper water.

In winter, they migrate far away from land to areas with open water.

Most belugas migrate to specific areas for feeding, **moulting**, and caring for their young.

Belugas rub their skin on shallow rocky areas in the summer to moult. Moulting happens when belugas get rid of the dead skin on their bodies.

Belugas are one of the many amazing animals found in Nunavut.

There are over 130 000 belugas in the Canadian Arctic! Have you ever seen a beluga?

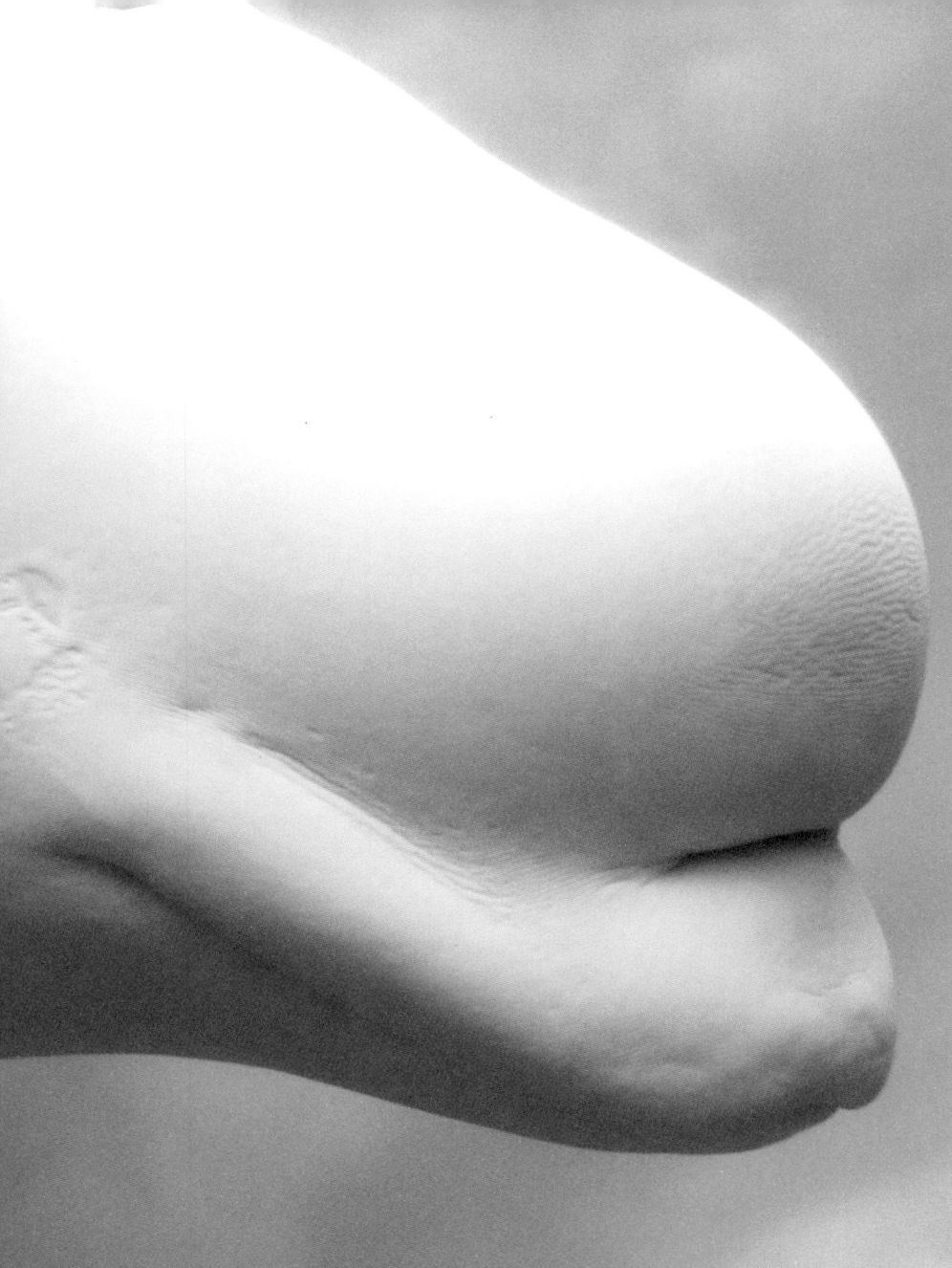

Glossary

blubber
a layer of fat beneath the skin of marine mammals. Blubber is used to keep marine mammals warm and as a source of energy.

crustacean
water animals that usually have a tough outer shell and no backbone.

marine environment
the seas and oceans, and the organisms that live there.

migrate
movement of animals from one area to another, usually with changing seasons.

moulting
a process of losing old hair or skin to allow for new hair or skin to grow.

predators
animals that hunt other animals.